# best man

poems by

Owen Lewis

DOS MADRES
2015

DOS MADRES PRESS INC.
P.O.Box 294, Loveland, Ohio 45140
www.dosmadres.com editor@dosmadres.com

Dos Madres is dedicated to the belief that the small press is essential to the vitality of contemporary literature as a carrier of the new voice, as well as the older, sometimes forgotten voices of the past. And in an ever more virtual world, to the creation of fine books pleasing to the eye and hand.

Dos Madres is named in honor of Vera Murphy and Libbie Hughes, the "Dos Madres" whose contributions have made this press possible.

Dos Madres Press, Inc. is an Ohio Not For Profit Corporation and a 501(c)(3) qualified public charity. Contributions are tax deductible.

Executive Editor: Robert J. Murphy

Illustration & Book Design: Elizabeth H. Murphy
www.illusionstudios.net

Typset in Adobe Garamond Pro & Pesky Phoenicians
ISBN 978-1-939929-35-8
Library of Congress Control Number: 2015939857

*First Edition*

ALSO BY OWEN LEWIS:

poetry

*March in San Miguel*
*Sometimes Full of Daylight*

poetry/multi-media

*New Pictures at an Exhibitio*
(with Seymour Bernstein)

essays

*Psychotherapies with Children:*
*Adapting the Psychodynamic Process*
(with Jack O'Brien, Dan Pilowsky)

# PREFACE & ACKNOWLEDGEMENTS

Although it took over thirty years to come to write *Best Man*, it is a story I needed to tell. Despite this long gestation, it was not until I was well into the writing of it that I first considered—why now, why now was I writing about a brother gone for three decades? An answer to the question came and worked itself into the poem "Introducing." How was I to explain this part of my life to someone new in my life, to my then future wife Susan Ennis. I thank her for this impetus, and for the love that sustains my writing.

A second answer to "why now" was my fortunate meeting and subsequent work with Edward Hirsch. On reading the first poem of the set, he suggested that within that one poem a cycle of poems was waiting to be written. Did he know? He knew. Over the next two to three months, the majority of these poems were written. His specific input on various poems was invaluable. But more than that, his deep understanding of the complexity, pain, and imperative of the extended elegy nurtured the entire process. To Ed, a gratitude that goes beyond words. The epigraph is from his *Gabriel.*

Deepest thanks as well to Martha Rhodes and Fran Quinn, who have been dedicated teachers, mentors, and friends; to my publisher Robert Murphy, who on first reading the set insisted it be published as a book of its own, and to Elizabeth Murphy for her haunting cover and book design; and my thanks also to friends and writers who have seen, heard, and helped versions along the way—Greg Egan, Paola Baccaglini, Carroll Joynes, Abby O'Neil, Boris Thomas, Matthew Biel, Dorothy Goldman, Nick Samaras, Anne-Marie Fyfe, Jim Tolan, Myra Shapiro, Yossi Yzraeli, Kate Daniels, Jeffrey Harrison, Rodney Jones, and Laure-Anne Bosselaar.

*Best Man* comprises twenty-three poems. Jason lived to be twenty-three. For my parents, now deceased, who did their utmost to sustain him, to my brother Arthur who shared Jason's life and has his own story to tell, and to the many, many families who have struggled in similar ways—this book is offered.

*for my brother Jason*

# CONTENTS

## *Prologue*



## *Best Man*

*Look closely and you will see*
*Almost everyone carrying bags*
*Of cement on their shoulders*

~ Edward Hirsch

# *Prologue*

## *Post-Script, Unwritten Letter*

Taking every memory that came to me like a hand in the dark,
sometimes leading, sometimes waiting to be led, sometimes grabbing
for your hand to wrestle

the night—or did you find me, brother, reaching between the planes
of the dark? When you were speaking, I wanted to know from where
what unfolded shadow,

and I made myself get up, scratch ink to paper like the children we were
digging through the backyard soil, determined to get to China,
the spot under the swings

where our feet whisked the ground before each pendulum soar, and if
we could rise out of the earth, we'd find our way through it . . .
if I could,

where do we go? We leave the house from the front door, along the walk
that curves across the lawn. The crimson king maple has just been planted,
a sapling

once staked against the wind, grown wide now giving lots of shade,
and the stones, as they were without wear, both these
and the marker.

At the end of the driveway, a mailbox, its red flag always up, unwaving.
Wherever you've been you'll have something to tell me. I expected
to know more.

*Best Man*

## *1. So,*

I am still mad at you.
Every week another call

from a pharmacy, a burnt-out Bronx
neighborhood, or Brooklyn.

Percocet, Dexedrine, shopping lists.
Benzo's. That last visit you took

my prescription pad, sold it.
I refused your calls.

From Florida. From the ICU.
Frantic, your girlfriend overdosed.

Our grandmother told me you were ok.
She cooked you a pair of fried eggs.

I've never known how to think
about your end, so, often I just don't.

## *2. Thaw*

I hate March—white flowers pushing
the edges, Mother traipsing us
around the yard to see those little blooms,
birthday presents—yours—she called them.

She's gone, too, and who's to celebrate
the scatter of white snowdrops?
They shame me, their strength,
each lifting a plaque of ice. The snow lies,

a smoothing of contours across the yard.
Now, a jagged branch, an elbow sticking through,
a poke in the side it prods what lurks,
what hides within any person's body as if,

from the start, that body's death note
were already written, Mother's cancer,
Father's failing lungs, so it's March 12th
at 7:32 pm, doesn't matter the year, the decade,

again the scatter of white pills across your bed.

## *3. En Route*

(Beth Israel Cemetery)

It doesn't seem to matter, visiting
or not. Who the hell's here?
So many people left pebbles near
to say hello. Not one for you.

Who's watching, a town
of relatives, on Ridgedale Avenue,
Cedar Knolls. Not my Xanadu.
En route to an aunt who remembers

and friends who don't. Can't
look at your name, staring,
the headline always blaring:
Found After Three Days.

Bellaire Motel, Miami, hundred degree
nights. The air a fever, coma
oozing from your eyes. No diploma
needed to read this dark. Your face

running off your cheeks, in rivulets.
Back home, the northern earth took hold,
hardened eyes to praise the cold,
and those who cried had ice for tears.

I'm here again, hello?
What muck! No one tending this ground.
After thirty years still sinking down,
as if, only now, inviting a stay.

There's nothing here, or tell me—

*Get the fuck away!*
You said—*Get away?*
You really told me to get away?

## *4. New Museum*

Even some parents wanted to know
what's here: fossil fish and old bones;
amethyst, lava stone and granite;

luna moths, scorpions, and cicadas;
coins from Timbuktu; letters from Russia;
five kinds of oak leaf, blackbird and seagull

feathers, bear-tooth, bear-claw, snake-skin;
formaldehyde-frog, dog-brain, calf-heart.
Three minutes to opening, kid brother

jumps the stairs, trips, collapses a leg
on the display table. Insects crushed,
cicada cracked in several pieces—

I'll be 29 when they next come
out of the earth. Heart and brain
lying next to each other on the floor.

Almost used to him ruining things.
Outside the garage I take down the sign:
*Line Forms Here* (with an arrow).

I would have let them in two by two,
ready to sail them to new worlds.

## 5. *Once,*

upon a time, in Convent Station,
a grandma brought a baby
to a new home, in a baby-blue
afghan she crocheted special.
Once upon a time, it's true,
the mother and brother, a pair,
stood by the front storm door,
looking out, a long wait
for the new baby to get there.
Like it was coming from a store.
Like a birthday present, only late.
The dad was parking the car,
on the street in front of the house,
Normandy Boulevard West,
when the grandma put the baby
into its mother's arms. The brother
waited his turn. He thought maybe
he'd have a friend. Told not to smother
it, he watched, waited so long to say—
I'm your brother, and, so, I'm . . .
I'm . . . long upon this time.

Too long upon this time.

## *6. Lingering Here*

(Beth Israel Cemetery)

And what of the family's soul,
Mother, as if you already knew
his disquieted soul won't find peace

in its orbit of earth, an empty satellite
fleeing the angels come to lead him
through the glare—his girlfriend

from King Street, also angel, on Sundays
in taffeta and gauze, flowing the makeshift
aisle at the county mall, a model

of wedding gowns. He was to be her escort
in a tux, a ruffled shirt, and we waited
till the store's metal grate rumbled shut.

His soul was already flying off,
off to his Italian birth mother, the one
he breach-busted out of, who gave him away.

She couldn't know him, but he'd know her
and call her by knocking a bottle of wine
to the floor. She'd curse, sweeping him in

among the dustpan pieces, and he, crying
as he again rushed off to answer his friend's
last call, entering that room to find it filled

with the night's blood, and crying home,
back to you, your balcony by the sea,
straddling the fourteenth-story ledge

leaning out, ready to fly—
and so—on a salty gust, into the sunset's
infant pink, the last crying beat of the gull's

wing, a stretch of mauve, a bruise.

## *7. The Line*

Like the dune fences
at the shore. Enough slats
to keep things together, but still
some sand pours through.

Remember how each year
we'd come back, have to learn
the beach all over again?
The wind still arranges hills.

The shipwreck, one year
on the beach, next, far out
on the sandbar. We traced
the fences that were almost

covered. A row of red nubbins
sticking through. The line
never a line. Our sticks
clacking as we raced.

## 8. *At The Devereux School*

We were once three kids. *Hey Jude,*
*Don't make it bad*—driving there, radio noise.
Where do I find him? *Anytime you feel the pain, refrain.*

Bare trees brooming the drive. Welcome?
They send me to the Somebody-Somebody Building.
Inside, a row of army cots stretching back in a warehouse

meant for raising chickens. He's fourteen, hunched on his bed,
back to me. *They're all whack here,* he says, as if I had just come
from the kitchen with a sandwich, roast beef, mayo, provolone.

Medicines making him heavy. He eats because there's nothing
else to do. I'm just out of college. It's dim, with the dark
laundry smell of twenty boys, the overhead fan stirring currents

of neglect. Anyone telling them to change their underwear?
I give him a Grateful Dead sweatshirt, but I'm shivering
and he gives me his black cardigan with his name-tag inside—

I keep it on till the spring. He reaches for a hug, distracted,
fingers the gold amulet on my neck. He's already taken so much
I just give it to him. He'll sell it later, now tucks it inside his shirt,

tilts his head to ask, embarrassed what he can't remember—
*chai*—as numbers meaning eighteen, as letters, life.
*Hey Jude, don't let me down!*

## *9. Advice*

(on the jailhouse steps, Court Place)

If you visit someone in jail,
hold onto the handrail.
You'll leave part of yourself there.
You can't actually give some
thing to the other person like
a pack of lifesavers or a note
from your pocket or some
dollars. There aren't window
bars you can reach through
to shake hands. It's plexiglass
with a circle of little holes so
what you leave has to pass
that barrier. It might be
a look that tries to be kind
but is really a lot of questions
that can't be answered. It's
not a bunch of words because
it's noisy and confused and
everybody else's words mix in.
It will be something from inside
of you like a lungful of air
you've brought from outside.
It could be spring and warm
and full of color or winter
that is crisp and ice-blue. But
when you pass this season on
you'll take a season in
that's full of very mean things
that will fill you up and be in-
side of you and make you think
you should be there too so you

won't think your time's up
until the guard taps your back
because twenty minutes are over
that seem like twenty days
and the doors close and you're
outside in the air of the season
you brought inside and what's
in and out or right and wrong
aren't clear and when you stop
at the deli for a coffee and tuna
sandwich you don't know how
you passed a bill to the cashier
or how she passed you change
and why she is smiling or how
your hand could lift the cup
past the barrier or the sandwich
right up to your open mouth.

## 10. *Nightlife*

One dancing bear in the spotlight—
where'd you learn that two-step?
*K-bum, thump. K-bum, thump.*
With me in your arms, you've got
to jiggle and waltz. Count of three,

then we whirl, dancing bear,
night to noon and back again?
Your breath is foul from rotten
meat. Your nostrils flare me
fresh in the cave of your furry hug.

Four fine claws skewer
my back, right along the spine.
With a roar and a shake give me
to the sun. With a soft meow
you lick the moon. Listening,

boogie-woogie, you're dancing
with my five limbs. Electrify the beat,
great bear, music of the spheres.
What glistening necklace loops
your collarbone? Your face is red.

## *11. Gutter Spill*

Gutter spill
gravel
under cheek and arm skin
tattoos a picture of night

after clock-stop
the bakery's yeast rises into the dawn

the sky so hungry it eats its own rising

sun
mid-morning visit
to a forty-second street shop
flowers painted on the walls waist high
with holes in each center
with sucking mouths on the other side
dicks grinding away at the wall-flowers

men adjusting themselves meander away

endless grids of sidewalk Port Authority
thirty-fourth street Path Station

to Hoboken to the Erie-Lack-
awanna old green trains
like a Lionel set we once played with

wicker seats flip direc-
tions make it hard to know what's coming
what's going and
your sleep is coma's trial run
when the conductor once Virginian bass-baritones

"Convent Station"
the words slap into a creviced shadow of sleep
knock you
out of the train
you fall
into a bevy of passing nuns

"Sisters of Mercy"
who happen to know your mother
and don't take you to the state hospital

"Greystone Park"
take you home because this is a town
a while longer
that you recognize

and recognizes you.

## *12. The Clamp Inside the Body*

Okay brother,
give me what you got.
A kick to the solar plexus.

You want to make it hurt.

There's a clamp in there,
like a surgeon's mistake.
Where I clamped it all off.

So many mistakes
are left in my body.
How many in yours?

I broke the phone
you called on. Broke my own
arm. Took notes, threw bits

in the air, as if a celebration.

Only the clamp is left.
Kick hard. Knock the air out.
Make it hurt.

Send stars into my head.
Take them back.
Stuff them into my mouth.

## *13. At The Payne Whitney Clinic*

Here is Miss K—in the fixed position of a wrought iron *S*
over the toilet, a frozen cry—*Help me decide*—a voice locked inside,
a solid fecal log hangs just touching the bowl's still water.

Mrs. M disimpacts eleven Louis Vuitton suitcases, folds, unfolds
twelve angora cardigan sets. Husband brings three more—
cranberry, ochre, and opaline—he gifts her goodbye.

Mr. Mike, fly-swatting his back, a field where insects breed,
centipedes eating millipedes, *God Save the Queen*, and poor Queenie,
closet-locked for her first five years, follows him

picking up carcasses, tucks them under the rows of her braids.
This is 1980, and Dr. L, that is me at twenty-nine,
trying to make sense of this world.

Dr. L must conduct group therapy, gathers Mrs. M, Mike,
Queenie, not K. Others come to show a healing wrist, a rope
burn. The room should be quiet, fills with street-noise. What engine?

What is back-firing? Dr. L can't tell who is speaking, who not.
His brother enters the room, but that's impossible. Two months ago,
at twenty-three, he overdosed. The doctor can't remember

his brother's name. Is he there, someplace among the many pages
of the roster? *The New York Times* on a breezy Sunday in Central Park,
*Help Wanted*, flies to the top of an oak. He reaches into the air,

the group quiets, reaching with him. So many arms, hands like nets
waving, slowly, synchronized. He must comfort them all.
Everyone. Or maybe he has. He can't push past his lips the words

murmuring in his throat and wonders how ventriloquists sing.

## *14. Hearing Him?*

*So you think you've called me up?*
*I've called on you.*
*The scratch*
*on your back. The way you must*
*think*
*about me when nostalgia*
*moves.*
*Not so, bubbeleh,*
*kiddo, hermano mio.*
*It's me*
*digging you out.*
*Interrupting.*
*Disrupting.*

*I can make the fork drop*
*from your hand,*
*the sun glare*
*right in your eye,*

*make your dick shrink*
*in the middle of oo-*
*la-lah love.*

*I'm a termite in the wood*
*of your brain. Calling 1-800-*
*exterminator.*
*Calling 911.*
*Calling*
*look at yourself in the mirror.*

*I am the shower mist.*

## *15. Contrite Today,*

and exhausted. Aren't you?

*You've just moved. Broadway and 101.*
*Why didn't you send me an announcement.*
*I knew anyway, saw you*

about to scald my mouth with tea.
You rushed to the spout, gathered
the steam in your arms and yanked
the heat into the air. Thank you.

*Big-mouth, know-it-all,*
*suddenly I wanted you to keep talking,*
*wanted to hear the way you put*
*things into words.*
*I was always taking them out,*
*taking what I could get. I'm tired.*
*Maybe it's time to make a deal,*
*draw a line. Between here and there.*

A line like the dune fences . . .

*Remember how each year . . .*

New hills had formed . . .

*Summer was a long time ago.*

## 16. *The Net*

The letters of your name in the air I reach for them with a net.
Good thing for the silver fireflies drifting through the evening,
I would have been thought mad. Oh Dear Brother—

old aunts are still bringing chocolates. I have swooped some up—
some silver kisses. Uncle Lou has cracked his hip. I want to tell
a story, say sorry, August dog days and all, you were wild,

I hooked you to the dog-run, barking at the afternoon and the kids,
their laughter, now with the net's long pole can't collect, or soothe
your face redder than sunburn. Silver letters from your name

escape the words I'd write—the night's evening is wide, and the net—
I've got some of Grandmother's letters here and a luna moth
tearing its wings flapping with blame—the net is getting full.

My cello's in there. Take it back, strings and bow. Dad's silver dollars
spent on cigarettes and gum. Oh Dad, who couldn't cry, his sides
cut and burst, slivered with a case of shingles rough as a fallen roof,

my arms so tired, the net so full, and Michael your friend cut himself
with a silver knife. His blood inks the sky darker yet, the night's evening
wide, the net so full, the more I swish the net, the more the moon fades.

How do I write when you hardly knew to read? A postman stalks
this sky, this wide dark sky. Here, this satchel, this burgeoning net.
Here, a letter of your name drifts into the vast night's evening

across acres of a flying cemetery, and the sky, a sky of migrating souls.
Oh the dark night's evening, and my net is full of silver holes.

## *17. Introducing*

So you'll be there, I'm sure.
Where, how, don't know.
A pea-face in my boutonniere?
Static in my bride's veil?

I've been trying to figure out
how to introduce you.
You didn't like the first wife.
She kept that nose in the air.

This one, you'll like. You will.
So, Jason meet Susan, Susan,
Jason. Under the *chuppah*
the Rabbi will call: *Yaacov ben Simcha.*

Like the angels—Jacob, son
of Happiness. Come with me.
Everyone, generations, will be
there. You'll ride on my shoulder—

Best Man!

## *18. Blackbird*

This morning, the hour of haze,
a blackbird called through my window
with some urgency. (I think it was you.)

I think he expected an answer.
Further back in the field I heard
a lot of bird back-and-forth.

This one made of himself a horn,
and whatever the sound of feathers
scraping the screen, he made.

He could've pecked in if he wanted.
I rose, and he flapped those wings
like a Jesus angel.

It was wrong to try to rise up, too.
He wanted me to stay in bed, back
in the hour of haze.

There he'd talk to me. So I tried,
rolled my eyes back but couldn't,
too eager, always, for the day.

Then came a full chorus of bird-blare
in perfect pitches, and through the screen
his single black arrow.

## *19. Summersong*

I heard my father down the hall, his calls for help echoing,
I rushed across the years to my mother. I heard my father.

She cried: *I want my grandmothers here. With me.* Her night-
gown fell, she flung herself to bed, breast bare and crying.

How mute my father, found her still mourning for my brother.
He longed to find her and there, did nothing, how mute

before this, my mother into the demented years, long after
she had died, hair of disheveled shocks, this my mother.

When I spoke she remembered her care, remembered
something deeply, as if a knife of fire when I spoke.

*Where are the cicadas? I'm a biologist. I've waited seventeen long years.*
*All the years in one song. Like a grandmother. Where are the cicadas?*

The stars fell from the sky, a copious fall, carcasses of light
on roofs, walls, mountains, down gutters of lava the stars fell.

With cicadas singing, the stars fell. I saw beyond the once
of dying, and birth, memory shed, singing again with cicadas.

## *20. Last Supper, Broadway Szechuan*

Three tiers of Polynesian
delight—the Pu-Pu
Platter! Eighteen pieces
plus one for good luck,
one for good health!
(Did you really order this?)
Egg rolls and spareribs
with fancy paper tails.
Clinking goblets, rummed
pineapple and passion fruit.
(Toasting without words.)
A rainbow of mini-umbrellas.
Shrimp in acrylic pink,
skewers of chicken dyed red,
a bouquet of sparklers
lighting our dark corner.

## *21. Where now*

do our hands clasp?

Between gravel path and granite,
each reaching for the other,
no longer turn away, the warm

and cold of it,
                              and Grandfather
turning his face toward the door,
the sun, the chill October breeze,
he closed his eyes, I did, too,
and eyes glowing red we talked
about making fall resolutions,
how many he had and I, none
back then, and in a soft laugh
said—as if I could have known
more; I remember that same
child swimming an August lake,
the sudden up-drift, a glacial spring
hitting me like a fist in the belly,
I kept going, kept going . . .
that same man, the frozen
sadness returning, ice-leaching,
eyes unwilling . . .

between gravel path and granite
brothers breaching
the warm and cold of it

reaching out . . .

## *22. . . . I place a pebble on his gravestone*

Jason Lewis

1957-1980

Beloved Son and Brother

## ABOUT THE AUTHOR

OWEN LEWIS's poetry has appeared in *The Mississippi Review, The Connecticut River Review, The Adirondack Review, The Four Way Review, The Cumberland Review* and other publications and received awards from *The Mississippi Review, The Connecticut River Review,* The Amherst Writers and Artists press, and The London School of Jewish Studies. He is the author of two collections of poetry, *March in San Miguel* and *Sometimes Full of Daylight.* He is also the co-author of the multi-media work *New Pictures at an Exhibition*, which received numerous concert performances. A physician and professor at Columbia University, he has also published widely in the professional literature. He currently teaches with the narrative medicine group at Columbia University and lectures on this work.

Books by Dos Madres Press

Mary Margaret Alvarado - *Hey Folly* (2013)
John Anson - *Jose-Maria de Heredia's Les Trophées* (2013),
*Time Pieces - poems & translations* (2014)
Jennifer Arin - *Ways We Hold* (2012)
Michael Autrey - *From The Genre Of Silence* (2008)
Paul Bray - *Things Past and Things to Come* (2006),
*Terrible Woods* (2008)
Ann Cefola - *Face Painting in the Dark* (2014)
Jon Curley - *New Shadows* (2009), *Angles of Incidents* (2012)
Grace Curtis - *The Shape of a Box* (2014)
Sara Dailey - *Earlier Lives* (2012)
Dennis Daly - *Nightwalking with Nathaniel-poems of Salem* (2014)
Richard Darabaner - *Plaint* (2012)
Deborah Diemont - *Wanderer* (2009), *Diverting Angels* (2012)
Joseph Donahue - *The Copper Scroll* (2007)
Annie Finch - *Home Birth* (2004)
Norman Finkelstein - *An Assembly* (2004), *Scribe* (2009)
Karen George - *Swim Your Way Back* (2014)
Gerry Grubbs - *Still Life* (2005), *Girls in Bright Dresses Dancing* (2010),
*The Hive-a book we read for its honey* (2013)
Richard Hague - *Burst, Poems Quickly* (2004),
*During The Recent Extinctions* (2012)
Ruth D. Handel - *Tugboat Warrior* (2013)
Pauletta Hansel - *First Person* (2007), *What I Did There* (2011)
Michael Heller - *A Look at the Door with the Hinges Off* (2006),
*Earth and Cave* (2006)
Michael Henson - *The Tao of Longing & The Body Geographic* (2010)
R. Nemo Hill - *When Men Bow Down* (2012)
W. Nick Hill - *And We'd Understand Crows Laughing* (2012)
Eric Hoffman - *Life At Braintree* (2008), *The American Eye* (2011),
*By The Hours* (2013)
James Hogan - *Rue St. Jacques* (2005)

Keith Holyoak - *My Minotaur* (2010), *Foreigner* (2012)
Nancy Kassell - *Text(isles)* (2013)
David M. Katz - *Claims of Home* (2011), *Stanzas on Oz* (2014)
Sherry Kearns - *Deep Kiss* (2013)
Burt Kimmelman - *There Are Words* (2007),
*The Way We Live* (2011)
Jill Kelly Koren - *The Work of the Body* (2014)
Ralph La Charity - *Farewellia a la Aralee* (2014)
Pamela L. Laskin - *Plagiarist* (2012)
Owen Lewis - *Sometimes Full of Daylight* (2013)
Richard Luftig - *Off The Map* (2006)
Austin MacRae - *The Organ Builder* (2012)
Mario Markus - *Chemical Poems-One For Each Element* (2013)
Patricia Monaghan - *Mary-A Life in Verse* (2014)
J. Morris - *The Musician, Approaching Sleep* (2006)
Rick Mullin - *Soutine* (2012), *Coelacanth* (2013),
*Sonnets on the Voyage of the Beagle* (2014)
Fred Muratori - *A Civilization* (2014)
Robert Murphy - *Not For You Alone* (2004),
*Life in the Ordovician* (2007), *From Behind The Blind* (2013)
Pam O'Brien - *The Answer To Each Is The Same* (2012)
Peter O'Leary - *A Mystical Theology of the Limbic Fissure* (2005)
Bea Opengart - *In The Land* (2011)
David A. Petreman - *Candlelight in Quintero-bilingual ed.* (2011)
Paul Pines - *Reflections in a Smoking Mirror* (2011),
*New Orleans Variations & Paris Ouroboros* (2013),
*Fishing on the Pole Star* (2014),
*Message from the Memoirist* (2014)
Samantha Reiser - *Tomas Simon & Other Poems* (2015)
William Schickel - *What A Woman* (2007)
David Schloss - *Behind the Eyes* (2005)
Don Schofield - *In Lands Imagination Favors* (2014)
Daniel Shapiro - *The Red Handkerchief and other poems* (2014)

Murray Shugars - *Songs My Mother Never Taught Me* (2011),
*Snakebit Kudzu* (2013)
Jason Shulman - *What does reward bring you but to bind you to Heaven like a slave? (2013)*
Maxine Silverman - *Palimpsest (2014)*
Lianne Spidel & Anne Loveland - *Pairings* (2012),
*Bird in the Hand* (2014)
Olivia Stiffler - *Otherwise, we are safe* (2013)
Carole Stone - *Hurt, the Shadow-the Josephine Hopper poems* (2013)
Nathan Swartzendruber - *Opaque Projectionist* (2009)
Jean Syed - *Sonnets* (2009)
Madeline Tiger - *The Atheist's Prayer* (2010),
*From the Viewing Stand* (2011)
James Tolan - *Red Walls* (2011)
Brian Volck - *Flesh Becomes Word* (2013)
Henry Weinfield - *The Tears of the Muses* (2005),
*Without Mythologies* (2008), *A Wandering Aramaean* (2012)
Donald Wellman - *A North Atlantic Wall* (2010),
*The Cranberry Island Series* (2012)
Sarah White - *The Unknowing Muse* (2014)
Anne Whitehouse - *The Refrain* (2012)
Martin Willetts Jr. - *Secrets No One Must Talk About* (2011)
Tyrone Williams - *Futures, Elections* (2004), *Adventures of Pi* (2011)
Kip Zegers - *The Poet of Schools* (2013)

www.dosmadres.com